Daddy, What is Love?

BY:

MICHAEL LEWIS, MD

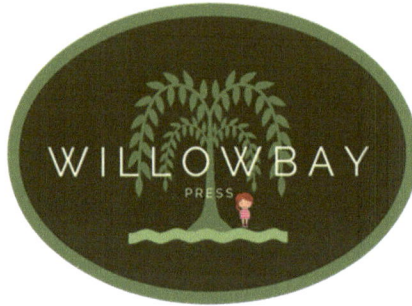

Willow Bay Press
7842 Valley Flores Dr.
West Hills, Ca 91364
www.willowbaypress.com
Printed in the United States of America

ISBN-13: 978-0692070628 (Willow Bay Press)
ISBN-10: 0692070621

For my sweet angel, Bailey

Bailey is a fun-loving, charismatic,
curious 7-year-old girl. She is in the first grade.
And like most first graders
she is curious about many things:

She is curious about the clouds.
She is curious about birds.

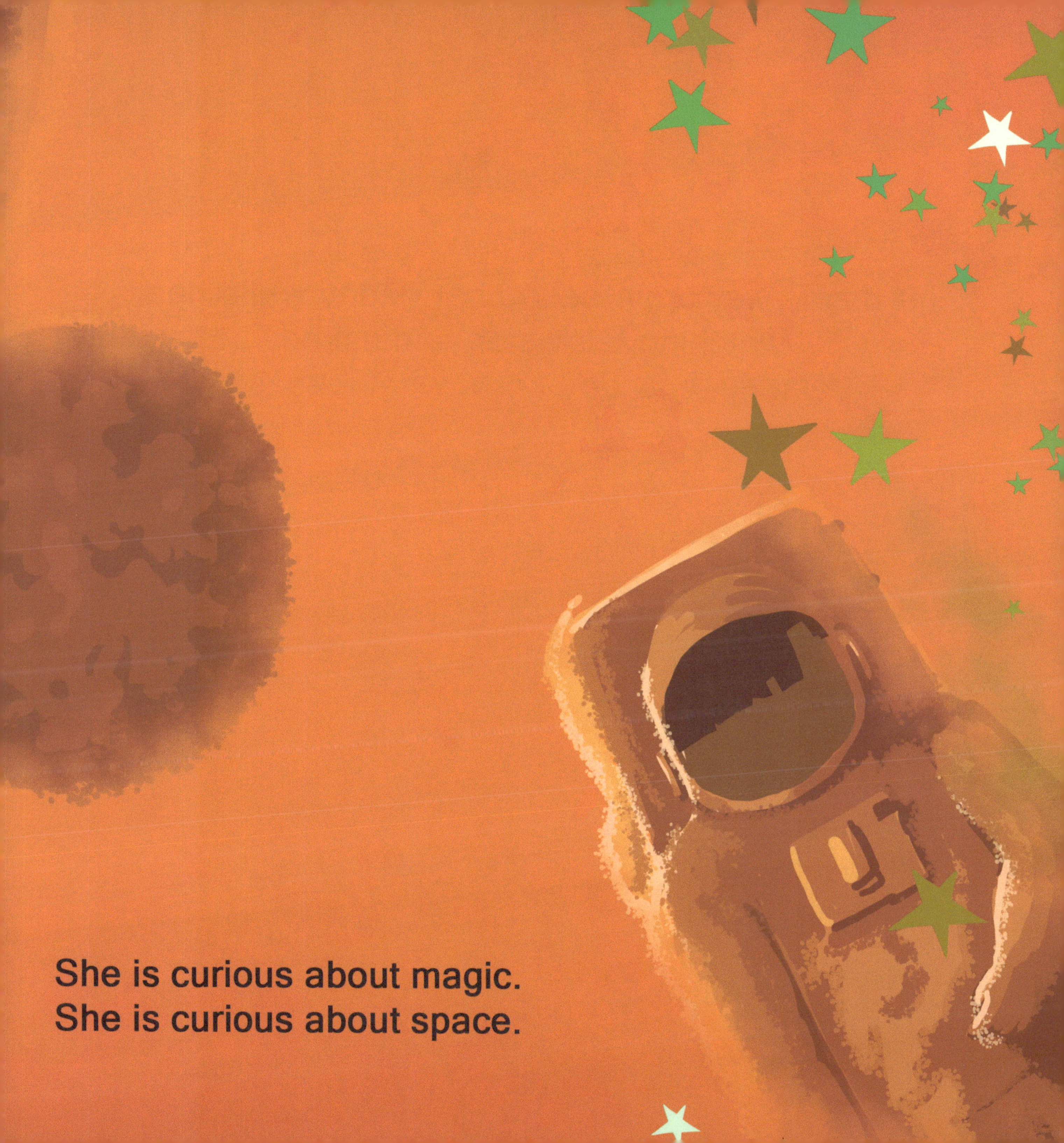

She is curious about magic.
She is curious about space.

One-day Bailey approached her daddy while he was
watching television and asked:
"Daddy, how do I know what love is?"

Bailey's daddy, turned off the television,
sat up, and asked, "Why honey?"
Bailey said, "Well daddy,
I like clouds and birds and magic and space,
but I don't luuvvvvvv them."

"I see," said daddy smiling.

Bailey continued, "I love you and mommy,
but how do I know?"
Daddy said, "That's a great question sweetheart.
Let's see if I can help you
understand."

Daddy brought Bailey up onto his lap,
pulled her into his chest and placed his nose
on her head and took a deep breath.

Daddy said, "When I smell your beautiful skin,
I feel a wonderful tingling sensation
all the way down to my toes,
as if it was raining stars
from the heavens all over me."

"Really daddy?" said Bailey.
"Yes, honey. Oh yes," said daddy
as he smiled and gazed into
Bailey's curious eyes.

"What else daddy?"

Daddy put his head back,
closed his eyes and pretended to snore.
He said, "When I'm asleep and
I am awakened by your gentle hug,
it's as if I am draped in the
warmest blanket on the coldest day."

"Really daddy?" said Bailey.
"Yes, honey. Oh yes," said daddy
as he smiled and gazed into
Bailey's curious eyes.
"What else daddy?"

Daddy looked at Bailey
with a mischievous grin
and started tickling her,
"When I hear the sound of your laughter,
it's like hearing my favorite song
playing over and over again."

"Really daddy?" said Bailey.
"Yes, honey. Oh yes," said daddy
as he smiled and gazed into
Bailey's curious eyes.

"What else daddy?"

Daddy looked down with a sad expression
and said, "When I'm at work
and I don't see you for a whole day,
I feel like part of me is missing."

"Really daddy?" said Bailey.
"Yes, honey. Oh yes," said daddy
as he smiled and gazed into
Bailey's curious eyes.

"What else daddy?"

Daddy looked at Bailey with a soft grin and said,
"And when you tell me you love me in your
sweet little voice, I can feel my heart beat faster,
pitter-patter, pitter-patter,
and I can feel my chest fill up
with feelings of joy…"

Bailey interrupted, "As if you were in love daddy?"
Her eyes widened.
"Yes, honey. Oh yes," said daddy
as he smiled and gazed into
Bailey's curious eyes.

Daddy said, "And that's how I know
I love you Bailey!"

PITT
PAT

With Bailey's eyes opened wide she said,
"Really daddy? Because when I lay on
your chest, I think you smell so good too.

And, when I try to wake you up with a
hug, it's because I want you to tickle me
because that's my favorite thing in the world!

And when you come home from work,
I get so excited that I want to stick to you like glue
because I missed you so much.

And when I tell you, 'I love you,'
I feel that same feeling in my chest too daddy!"
Bailey says surprised.
"Does that mean I love you, daddy?"

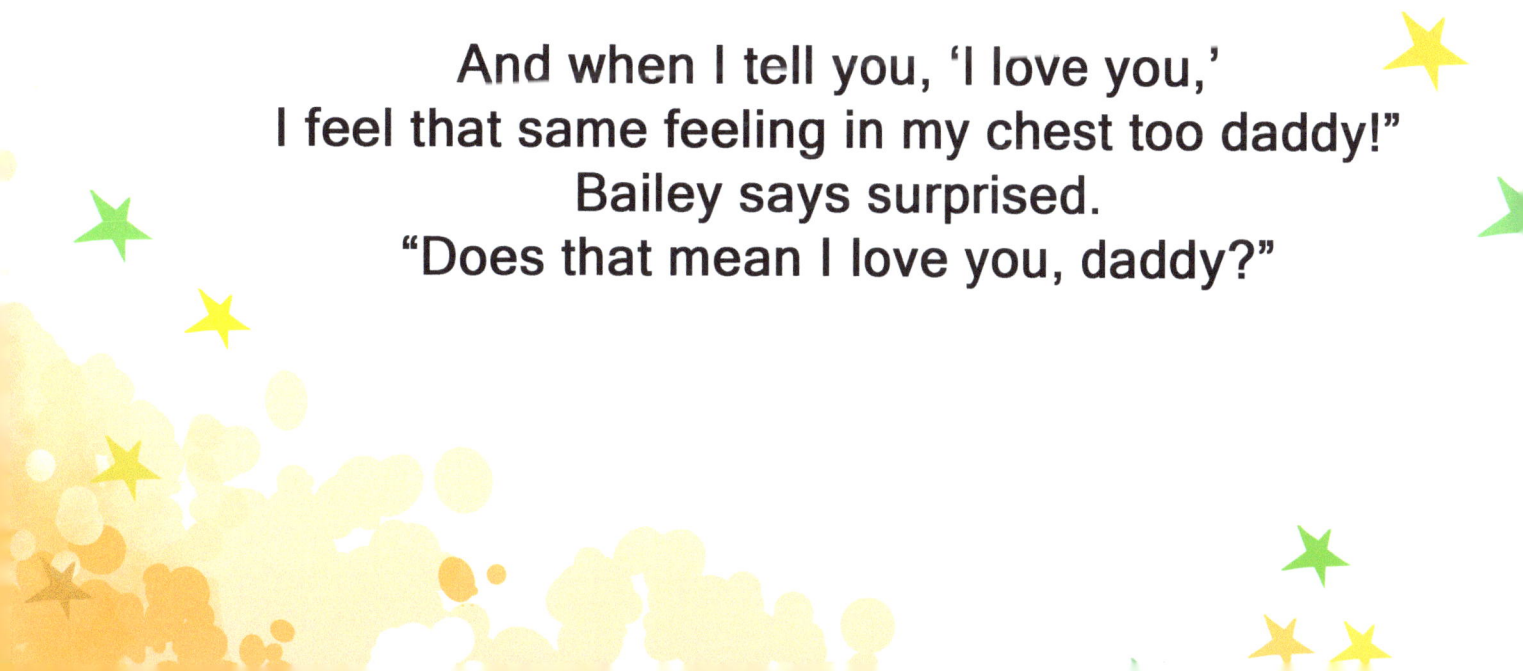

Daddy, gently rubbed Bailey's cheek
with his thumb and said,
"If you feel all those things my love,
what do you think?"

Bailey looked at daddy
and caressed his cheek and said,
"I love you too daddy...
I know it for sure."